Stark County District Library
Community Center Branch
1400 Sherrick Road SE
Canton, OH  44707
330.453.8042 OCT - - 2007
www.starklibrary.org

W9-BIV-833

DISCARDED

# WEEKLY WR READER®
## EARLY LEARNING LIBRARY

LET'S READ
ABOUT
*Animals*

# Kangaroos

## by Kathleen Pohl

**Reading consultant:** Susan Nations, M.Ed.,
author/literacy coach/consultant
in literacy development

Please visit our web site at: **www.garethstevens.com**
**For a free color catalog describing Weekly Reader® Early Learning Library's list**
**of high-quality books, call 1-877-445-5824 (USA) or 1-800-387-3178 (Canada).**
**Weekly Reader® Early Learning Library's fax: (414) 336-0164.**

**Library of Congress Cataloging-in-Publication Data**

Pohl, Kathleen.
  Kangaroos / by Kathleen Pohl.
    p. cm. — (Let's read about animals)
  Includes bibliographical references and index.
  ISBN-13: 978-0-8368-7817-2 (lib. bdg.)
  ISBN-13: 978-0-8368-7824-0 (softcover)
  1. Kangaroos—Juvenile literature.  I. Title.
  QL737.M35P64   2007
  599.2'22—dc22                    2006030867

This edition first published in 2007 by
**Weekly Reader® Early Learning Library**
A Member of the WRC Media Family of Companies
330 West Olive Street, Suite 100
Milwaukee, WI 53212 USA

Copyright © 2007 by Weekly Reader® Early Learning Library

Editor: Dorothy L. Gibbs
Art Direction: Tammy West
Cover design and page layout: Kami Strunsee
Picture research: Diane Laska-Swanke

Picture credits: Cover, title © Ferrero-Labat/Auscape; pp. 5, 7, 15, 19 © Jean-Paul Ferrero/Auscape;
p. 9 Kami Strunsee/© Weekly Reader® Early Learning Library; p. 11 © Graham Robertson/Auscape;
p. 13 © Owen Newman/naturepl.com; pp. 17, 21 © John Cancalosi/Auscape

All rights reserved. No part of this book may be reproduced, stored in a retrieval system,
or transmitted in any form or by any means, electronic, mechanical, photocopying,
recording, or otherwise, without the prior written permission of the copyright holder.

Printed in the United States of America

1 2 3 4 5 6 7 8 9 10 10 09 08 07 06

# Note to Educators and Parents

Reading is such an exciting adventure for young children! They are beginning to integrate their oral language skills with written language. To encourage children along the path to early literacy, books must be colorful, engaging, and interesting; they should invite the young reader to explore both the print and the pictures.

The *Let's Read About Animals* series is designed to help children read and learn about the special characteristics and behaviors of the intriguing featured animals. Each book is an informative nonfiction companion to one of the colorful and charming fiction books in the *Animal Storybooks* series.

Each book in the *Let's Read About Animals* series is specially designed to support the young reader in the reading process. The familiar topics are appealing to young children and invite them to read — and reread — again and again. The full-color photographs and enhanced text further support the student during the reading process.

In addition to serving as wonderful picture books in schools, libraries, homes, and other places where children learn to love reading, these books are specifically intended to be read within an instructional guided reading group. This small group setting allows beginning readers to work with a fluent adult model as they make meaning from the text. After children develop fluency with the text and content, the books can be read independently. Children and adults alike will find these books supportive, engaging, and fun!

— Susan Nations, M.Ed., author/literacy coach/
consultant in literacy development

You might see a **kangaroo** at a zoo.  Look for a furry animal that has big back feet and hops!

Kangaroos can hop very fast. Sometimes, they look like they are flying!

There are many kinds of
kangaroos.  They all come from
**Australia** (aw-STRAY-lee-ah).
The map shows where red
kangaroos and gray kangaroos
live in the wild.

**Australia**

**Tasmania**

## Map Key

- places red kangaroos live
- places gray kangaroos live
- places red and gray kangaroos live

9

Some kangaroos are very small.  Others may be very tall.  Red kangaroos are the biggest of all!

red kangaroos

Sometimes, kangaroos fight.
They look like they are boxing!

Kangaroos live in groups called **mobs**. They rest most of the day. It is too hot to move around!

At night, kangaroos move around a lot. They like to eat at night. Kangaroos eat grass and leaves.

The body of a newborn kangaroo has a shape like a jelly bean.  The baby is called a **joey** (joh-ee).

**newborn joey**

A joey grows inside its mother's **pouch** for many months.  Then, it peeks out.  Welcome to the world, little joey!

joey

pouch

# Glossary

**Australia** — an island continent in the southern half of the world

**joey** — a baby animal that grows in its mother's pouch, such as a kangaroo or a koala

**kangaroo** — a large animal from Australia that hops and has a pouch on its belly for its babies

**mobs** — groups of kangaroos

**pouch** — the special pocket that kangaroos and some other animals have on their bellies and use to hold their babies

# For More Information

## Books

*Jumping Kangaroos.* Pull Ahead Books (series). Michelle Levine (Lerner Publications)

*The Kangaroo.* Life Cycles (series). Diana Noonan (Chelsea Clubhouse)

*A Kangaroo Joey Grows Up.* Baby Animals (series). Joan Hewett (Carolrhoda Books)

*The Kangaroos' Great Escape.* Animal Storybooks (series). Rebecca Johnson (Gareth Stevens)

## Web Site

Our Animals on the Ground: Kangaroos

*www.abc.net.au/schoolstv/animals/KANGAROOS.htm*

Read the fascinating facts and look at the fabulous photos to learn more about kangaroos.

**Publisher's note to educators and parents:** Our editors have carefully reviewed this Web site to ensure that it is suitable for children. Many Web sites change frequently, however, and we cannot guarantee that a site's future contents will continue to meet our high standards of quality and educational value. Be advised that children should be closely supervised whenever they access the Internet.

# Index

# About the Author

**Kathleen Pohl** has written and edited many children's books. Among them are animal tales, rhyming books, retold classics, and the forty-book series *Nature Close-Ups*. Most recently, she authored the Weekly Reader® Early Learning Library series *Where People Work*. She also served for many years as top editor of *Taste of Home* and *Country Woman* magazines. She and her husband, Bruce, live in the middle of beautiful Wisconsin woods and share their home with six goats, a llama, and all kinds of wonderful woodland creatures.